SandCastle

Dollars & Cents

Let's Add
Coins

Kelly Doudna

Consulting Editor Monica Marx, M.A./Reading Specialist

ABDO
Publishing Company

Published by SandCastle™, an imprint of ABDO Publishing Company, 4940 Viking Drive, Edina, Minnesota 55435.

Credits
Edited by: Pam Price
Curriculum Coordinator: Nancy Tuminelly
Cover and Interior Design and Production: Mighty Media
Photo Credits: Hemera, PhotoDisc

Library of Congress Cataloging-in-Publication Data

Doudna, Kelly, 1963-
    Let's add coins / Kelly Doudna.
        p. cm. -- (Dollars & cents)
    Includes index.
    Summary: Shows how to use addition to find out whether the coins two people have are enough to pay for various items and looks at different coins, from a penny to a half dollar.
    ISBN 1-57765-896-5
    1. Money--Juvenile literature. 2. Addition--Juvenile literature. [1. Money. 2. Addition.] I. Title. II. Series.

HG221.5 .D652 2002
640'.42--dc21

                                                                    2002071183

SandCastle™ books are created by a professional team of educators, reading specialists, and content developers around five essential components that include phonemic awareness, phonics, vocabulary, text comprehension, and fluency. All books are written, reviewed, and leveled for guided reading, early intervention reading, and Accelerated Reader® programs and designed for use in shared, guided, and independent reading and writing activities to support a balanced approach to literacy instruction.

Let Us Know

After reading the book, SandCastle would like you to tell us your stories about reading. What is your favorite page? Was there something hard that you needed help with? Share the ups and downs of learning to read. We want to hear from you! To get posted on the ABDO Publishing Company Web site, send us email at:

sandcastle@abdopub.com

SandCastle Level: Transitional

Coins are money.

one penny = 1¢

 one nickel = 5¢

 one dime = 10¢

 one quarter = 25¢

 one half-dollar = 50¢

We use coins to pay for things.

Let's see what we can buy.

The pencil costs 9¢.
9¢ = 9 pennies

Lisa has 6 pennies.

Mark has 3 pennies.

Do they have enough
to buy the pencil?

Let's add.
6 + 3 = 9

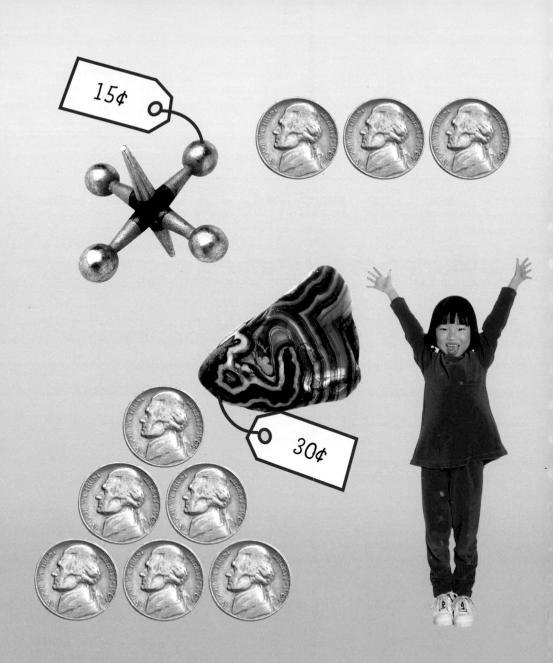

The jack costs 15¢.
15¢ = 3 nickels

The stone costs 30¢.
30¢ = 6 nickels

How many nickels
does Yuki need altogether?

Let's add.
3 + 6 = 9

The pencil sharpener costs 40¢.
40¢ = 8 nickels

Sue has 3 nickels.

John has 5 nickels.

Do they have enough
to buy the pencil sharpener?

Let's add.
3 + 5 = 8

The orange costs 50¢.
50¢ = 5 dimes

The apple costs 30¢.
30¢ = 3 dimes

How many dimes
does Bob need altogether?

Let's add.
5 + 3 = 8

The ice-cream cone costs $1.75.
$1.75 = 7 quarters

Nicki has 3 quarters.

Al has 4 quarters.

Do they have enough
to buy the ice-cream cone?

Let's add.
3 + 4 = 7

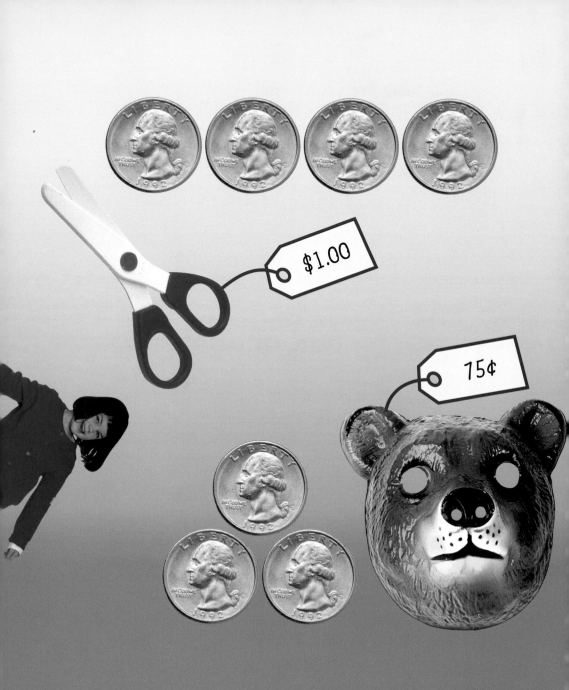

The scissors cost $1.00.
$1.00 = 4 quarters

The bear mask costs 75¢.
75¢ = 3 quarters

How many quarters
does Ann need altogether?

Let's add.
4 + 3 = 7

$3.00

The sunglasses cost $3.00.
$3.00 = 6 half-dollars

Liz has 3 half-dollars.

Jay has 3 half-dollars.

Do they have enough
to buy the sunglasses?

Let's add.
3 + 3 = 6

What are these coins called?

How much are they worth?

one penny = 1¢
one nickel = 5¢
one dime = 10¢
one quarter = 25¢
one half-dollar = 50¢

Index

Glossary

jack   a metal playing piece used in the game of jacks

mask   a covering worn over the face as a disguise

pencil sharpener   a tool used to shape the end of a pencil into a point

scissors   a sharp tool with two blades used for cutting

sunglasses   glasses that protect your eyes from the sun

About SandCastle™

A professional team of educators, reading specialists, and content developers created the SandCastle™ series to support young readers as they develop reading skills and strategies and increase their general knowledge. The SandCastle™ series has four levels that correspond to early literacy development in young children. The levels are provided to help teachers and parents select the appropriate books for young readers.

Emerging Readers
(no flags)

Beginning Readers
(1 flag)

Transitional Readers
(2 flags)

Fluent Readers
(3 flags)

These levels are meant only as a guide. All levels are subject to change.

To see a complete list of SandCastle™ books and other nonfiction titles from ABDO Publishing Company, visit **www.abdopub.com** or contact us at:

4940 Viking Drive, Edina, Minnesota 55435 • 1-800-800-1312 • fax: 1-952-831-1632